ASANA

A PLAY IN THREE ACTS

BILL MARSHALL

Afram Publications (Ghana) Limited

Published by:
Afram Publications (Ghana) Limited
P.O. Box M18
Accra, Ghana
Bill Marshall © 2013

Tel: +233 302 412 561, +233 244 314 103
E-mail: sales@aframpubghana.com
             publishing@aframpubghana.com
Website: www.aframpubghana.com

Cover illustration by Hawa Nikai-Olai

First Published 2013
ISBN: 9964-70-172-1

DEDICATION

TO MARTIN OBIRI

APPRECIATION

I thank my wife and children who supported me in
diverse ways to continue writing.
My deepest appreciation goes to Mary Dickson, who
patiently spent hours on the computer towards the
completion of this work.

CHARACTERS

ABEREWA: Called Mena, an old woman and a widow. She is blind.

THE SPIRIT: The hovering ghost of her dead husband.

ANIMA: Their daughter. A fish monger.

ABEKU: Their son. A labourer at the Elmina Castle.

ASANA: A slave girl.

TAKYI: A fisherman and a member of the Asafo Company, in love with Anima.

ACT ONE

The play takes place in the seaside town of Elmina, also known as Edina, towards the end of the 16th century. The scene is a household not far from the Elmina Castle. There are four rooms; the room upstage right is used as a store room for fish and other household items. Behind this room is the area for fish smoking. (Not seen by audience.)

The next room is Anima's bedroom. The room on the upstage left belongs to Abeku and down of this is Aberewa's bedroom.

The cooking area is on the right of stage and is made up of a simple shed and a low wall. Down of it leads into the street. There are cooking utensils and a big earthenware pot for storing water. On it is a calabash. There are some chairs lying about.

Time is late afternoon.

When the curtains open, we see Aberewa sitting in front of her room threading beads from a big calabash on her laps. She is blind but her eyelids are permanently open.
Spirit walks onto the stage and goes to peep at what Aberewa is doing. He is clad in a loose white jumper, large white knickerbockers and a white fisherman's cap to match. He is nimble in his gaits.

Anima enters the stage from the backyard carrying a basket of

*fish and enters the store room. She returns holding the empty
basket and one fish which she starts eating. As she goes to
inspect Aberewa's work, the spirit moves away.
(The other characters in the play do not see or hear the spirit.)*

ABEREWA: Have you finished?

ANIMA: No, there is one more basket of fish to
smoke because I had to go and fetch
firewood before starting.

ABEREWA: And you've started eating the fish
already.

ANIMA: Oh! Mena. I am just tasting it. Why, do
you want some?

ABEREWA: No, Anima. I'm not hungry. Why don't
you go and finish with the smoking?
You've spent too much time already
today.

ANIMA: I know… I know Mena. It's because Esi,
who works with me, couldn't come
today.

ABEREWA: And why, may I ask?

ANIMA: Because she is pregnant, and when you
are pregnant there are days you don't
feel too good.

ABEREWA: (*Sarcastically*) Oh, is that so? I don't know

3

	if you have that experience yourself…… *(She pauses for the sarcasm to sink in.)* And is this going to be her first child?
ANIMA:	No, Mena. I've told you, this will be her second child. Child number two…… Mena
ABEREWA:	Oh, is that so? And she is of the same age as you and you have not even started your child number one?
ANIMA:	Now, now, now, Mena, don't bring that all up again. I don't want to have a baby until I am properly married.
SPIRIT:	*(Bored by the conversation.)* Oh women and babies!

(He sits down on the floor cross-legged, Buddhist fashion.)

ABEREWA:	So why don't you get married? Takyi is a nice man and he is a good fisherman like your father.
ANIMA:	If he marries me, he will take me away and who is going to look after you?
ABEREWA:	Anima, you are using me as an excuse. If your father were alive, he would have given you a man to marry by now but he is not.
ANIMA:	Yes Mena, my father is not alive. He is dead and you are blind, so you need

4

	somebody to look after you and that somebody is me. If I get married, who is going to look after you?
SPIRIT:	They think I am dead. Yes, I am dead alright but my spirit is very much alive. I am a spirit with more capacity as a body than any mortal. It's a pity they can't see me and when I speak they can't hear me. Otherwise I can tell my wife what to do to cure her blindness. But what's the use, she can't see me and she can't hear me.
ABEREWA:	God will provide. He always provides for the needy. Look at me, I used to go far away in the East to towns near the big river to buy these beads, then I became blind and I couldn't go anymore.
SPIRIT:	That's what they call river blindness. Oh, what's the point; they can't hear me. *(He goes out.)*
ABEREWA:	But now, they travel all the way from there to Edina to bring me the beads to sell for them. What is more, even though I am blind, I can still thread these beads like I used to. That's how nature works. Besides, if you get married and go away, your brother will be here.
ANIMA:	He is a man. He cannot take care of you properly.

ABEREWA: Ah, but he will get married and his wife will come and live in this house and that woman will take care of me.

ANIMA: But that woman.....that woman......when is that woman coming? My brother goes about sleeping with so many women, and he brings a new woman to this house every day. Perhaps you don't know, but my brother doesn't keep to one woman. He is a real goat.

ABEREWA: Men are always like that until they settle.

ANIMA: Let me go and attend to the fish before they get burnt. Besides, these days the vultures worry me. They come in their numbers wanting to share the fish with me. Oh, these vultures.

(Anima takes the basket and goes to the backyard. Aberewa continues threading the beads in silence. After a while, we hear the boom of a canon-blast in the distance. Aberewa jumps at the sound and spills the beads on the floor. Anima rushes onto the stage from the backyard.)

ANIMA: Oh Mena, you've spilled the beads. If you keep on dropping that calabash it will crack.

ABEREWA: They fired the big gun.

ANIMA: Yes, I heard it but you have spilled the

6

beads, precious beads.

ABEREWA: Anima, you don't understand. These white people……..those Portuguese at the Elmina Castle are firing the big guns again.

ANIMA: Yes, Mena, it means that the slave ship is leaving today. They are taking a new batch of slaves away.

ABEREWA: Those people are not slaves. They are precious Africans, more precious than these beads.

ANIMA: Mena, they have been sending them away for years, why should that upset you now? Here, sit down and relax.

(She sits her mother down, continues to pick the beads and returns the beads and calabash to her. The spirit glides in and watches the scene thoughtfully.)

ABEREWA: It is not possible to relax when I hear those big guns. When your father disappeared at sea, it was these same big guns that were fired that killed the fishermen. I find it difficult to forget, Anima, I find it quite impossible to forget.

SPIRIT: *(Almost to himself.)* I don't blame her. It is difficult to forget me but the fact is that,

7

the guns that hit our boat and killed all five of us were fired from the ship and not those big guns from the castle, those canons. The captain of that ship thought we were an enemy boat; evildoers always fear their own shadows. We were only fishermen returning from sea that night...........

ANIMA: Now Mena, you try and forget it and continue with the beads. I will take them to the market tomorrow.

ABEREWA: I'm trying. I will try. Anima, have you ever sought to find out why the bodies of four of those fishermen were washed ashore, but up to now, some two years after that incident, after those big guns were fired, your father's body has not been found? *(Now near tears.)* Now he has not been buried and his soul will know no rest but floats around like a wandering spirit haunting people.

SPIRIT: Oh no, I'm not a haunting ghost. I am a happy spirit and I like it. I don't need any resting place. I like my present habit, free of time, free of space. I can access knowledge anytime and all information comes to me easily.

ANIMA: Mena, we all feel like you do, but the

funeral rites were performed two years ago, so we should all relax and live our normal lives.

ABEREWA: *(Vehemently)* Anima don't talk like that. How can you say the funeral rites have been performed when you did not see any dead body? Now we do not know if your father is dead or alive. So how can you say we should forget it and live our normal lives?

ANIMA: But Mena, we all know that my father is dead.

ABEREWA: But….where….is…the…body? It means that his soul still knows no peace and has been floating around like a wandering spirit. That worries me. Anima, you don't understand, but that man was my husband.

ANIMA: Mena, don't make me cry. Let me go and attend to the fish before they get burnt.

(She disappears into the background.)

SPIRIT: *(With a sigh)* Sensible girl. If only your mother knew that I was around her all the time, she would take some comfort, but as spirit, I am as free as a bird. I can get to any place that I want to, see all that I want to see and learn all that I want to learn.

That castle sitting there at the beach called Elmina Castle is a slave castle. The Portuguese built it under pretences. Now nobody knows that history but I have found out because I am a spirit. I can delve into history, literature, politics and even religion. And the Portuguese are Christians. And I have learnt all about that religion. That castle sitting up there was built in 1482. It is as old as that, and now in this 16th century, they are using it as a slave castle, when they should have been using it in trading gold. That makes me angry.

(He gets up angrily and walks away.)
(Anima brings a basket of fish into the store room.)

ABEREWA: Have you finished?

(Anima comes out.)

ANIMA: What did you say?

ABEREWA: I asked if you had finished.

ANIMA: Yes, now I have to put out the fire and tidy up the place. These vultures, these vultures... *(She goes back into the backyard.)*

(Abeku enters the house followed by the slave girl. She hesitates before entering the house. She is clad in an oversized army bush shirt. She is tall and slim. She is about 19 years old. She walks with a conspicuous limp. She is wearing a large copper earring in one ear.)

ABEREWA: Abeku, have you closed from work already?

ABEKU: Yes, Mena

ABEREWA: But you are not alone.

ABEKU: That's true Mena. But how do you know, you can't see.

ABEREWA: Don't talk like a fool, Abeku. I cannot see but I can hear.

ABEKU: I brought somebody.

ABEREWA: Ooooooooooo?

ABEKU: She is a woman.

ABEREWA: Ooooo? Another girlfriend? *(Raising her voice)* Abeku why don't you settle down and get married? What is wrong with you and your sister?

ABEKU: Mena, Mena, this is not another girlfriend. Why don't you wait for me to tell you about her?

ABEREWA: Alright, Abeku. You can start by telling

11

me why the woman you brought to this house is limping like that.

ABEKU: But Mena, how do you know she is limping, you can't see her.

ABEREWA: You are being foolish again, Abeku. I have ears. I can hear her footsteps.

ABEKU: Well she is a slave girl. She is from the castle.

(To the slave girl) This is my mother. People call her Aberewa which simply means 'old woman', but we her children call her Mena which means 'my mother'.

ABEREWA: *(Surprised)* What! A slave girl from the castle?

ABEKU: Yes Mena. You heard the big guns a while ago. That was the slave ship leaving.

ABEREWA: Yes, yes, I heard those big guns. They were going boom! Boom! Boom!

(Anima comes in from the backyard and is startled at the sight of the slave girl.)

ANIMA: *(Startled)* Oh dear!

ABEREWA: Don't worry Anima; this is not another girlfriend of your brother. She is a slave girl from the castle.

ASANA: *(Raising her voice in anger)* I am not a slave girl! I was not born a slave. You should not call me a slave. I was born a free person like everybody else and given a name. My name is Asana. Do you hear that? My name is Asana!

(All are surprised at this sudden outburst from the slave girl. The spirit walks in in a hurry. He sees the slave girl and stops in his tracks.)

ABEREWA: Anima, why don't you give her some water?

(As Anima fetches water for her, Abeku finds a chair for her to sit down and goes into his room. She drinks it and heaves a sigh of relief.)

ABEREWA: *(With deliberate emphasis on the name)* Ah, Asana. You must have come from the north.

ASANA: Yes, beyond the borders of this land

ABEREWA: And you are a twin?

ASANA: Yes, we are twins.

ABEREWA: Where is your twin sister?

ASANA: He is a boy. He is called Fuseini.

ABEREWA: Oh, so what happened?

ASANA: They came and captured us from our

village. It was me, my twin brother and my father.

ABEREWA: What happened to them?

ASANA: My father died on the way….and…and *(near tears)* now they have taken my brother away with the slave ship. We walked a long way. It must have been for several weeks, perhaps months, even years. I lost count of time. I don't even know what killed my father. He was ill when they came and took us from the village. So he wasn't that strong. When he died on the way, they left his body for the wild animals. So now, I only have my twin brother, but they have taken him on the ship.

ABEREWA: Sorry to hear that Asana. Why did they leave you behind?

ASANA: *(Angrily)* Because I was pregnant!

ABEREWA: What! Who made you pregnant?

ASANA: It is the Governor.

(Anima takes a chair and sits down.)

ANIMA: Now this is becoming more interesting. You mean the Portuguese governor at the Castle made love to you and made you pregnant?

14

SPIRIT: That amounts to rape. Rape is a criminal offence in Portugal.

(The spirit then sits on the floor, crosses his legs Buddhist fashion and listens.)

ABEREWA: Were you having an affair with him?

ASANA: No! No! No!

ABEREWA: Then what happened? Do you want to talk about it?

ASANA: Well, when we arrived, they separated us from the men and put us in a separate dungeon. One day, I wanted to go to my twin brother. We've been together since childhood, so I wanted to go to him. The guards would not let me, so they forced me back into the dungeon. The Governor saw me fighting with the guards so he asked them to bring me to him. He asked the guards to strip me naked. He looked at me and asked them to take me down and give me a bath.

ABEREWA: Then what happened?

ASANA: They took me back to him and he raped me. He repeated it several times.

SPIRIT: That's obscene. That's criminal.

ASANA: So I became pregnant. I wanted to die.

	I wanted to get that worm out of my stomach. I hit my head against the wall. I tried to kill myself but the guards wouldn't let me. They put me in chains and tied one leg to some big iron ball.
SPIRIT:	Cannon ball.
ABEREWA:	And that's why you limp the way you limp? Your ankle must be sore.
ASANA:	Yes, it hurts so much.
ABEREWA:	We will take care of that leg. Now tell me Asana, what happened to your mother?
ASANA:	She was not in the village when they came. At that time, she had gone to the farm to bring some foodstuff. Now, I don't know what happened to her. I wish I could be with her. I am sure she needs me now wherever she is. I am sure she is crying over us. Now, I don't know what to do with myself. All I know is, I am not going to have that white man's baby. I am going to make sure that I destroy it in my belly.
ABEREWA:	You should not talk like that Asana.
ASANA:	I think I should, that man raped me and destroyed my purity. Now I feel so dirty and impure. I keep vomiting all the time. Why should I bear him a child? Now I

16

don't even know where my brother is because they took him away.

SPIRIT: That's easy, I can find out. Now where is that ship......that slave ship........?

(He leaves the stage. Abeku emerges from his room. He is wearing a different shirt.)

ABEREWA: We will have to talk about this. Now, you are going to stay in this house. You are my child.

ABEKU: *(With some relief)* Well, well, well. That settles it. Now, I am going to town.

ANIMA: No, no, no. you can't leave the girl here alone. After all, you brought her here.

ABEKU: Ah! But Mena says she can stay with us.

ANIMA: That's what she said, but where does she sleep?

ABEKU: You are not suggesting she sleeps in my room? After all, she is already pregnant, if you know what I mean.

ANIMA: Didn't you know that before?

ABEKU: Of course I knew that before but it was better to bring her home than just to leave her in the streets. What's more, the Governor said I should take her out and look after her. At least, he was humane.

ASANA: *(Cynically)* Huh? Some Portuguese humanity!

ABEKU: Look at her. The Governor gave her his own shirt to put on. She is now better than the way she was at the castle.

ANIMA: Well, I can imagine. Having made her pregnant, it's only natural that he should seek for her welfare. Now, we have to give her proper clothing. This army shirt looks ridiculous on her.

ABEKU: Thank you, my dear, dear sister. So she will sleep in your room then.

ANIMA: Yes.

ABEREWA: That settles it.

ABEKU: Now, can I go out to town?

ANIMA: You can please yourself.

ABEKU: I'll see you later.

ANIMA: Why don't you give yourself some rest? Do you want to sleep with every woman in this town?

ABEKU: Ooh Anima, Anima why don't you leave me alone?

(Takyi walks onto the stage. He is well built and has rugged manners. He sniffs the air and smiles.)

TAKYI: Ah, I smell a good smell in this house.

ANIMA: Now Takyi, what do you smell?

TAKYI: I smell fish. Freshly smoked fish. Don't forget I am a fisherman and we fishermen like to smell the smell of freshly smoked fish.

ANIMA: Takyi, you can cut out that fisherman talk and greet Aberewa.

(He greets Aberewa.)

TAKYI: My greetings Aberewa, may the gods give you their blessings.

ABEREWA: Thank you. Oh, thank you Takyi.

TAKYI: Oh, I just came to confirm what we have heard.

ABEREWA: What have you heard?

TAKYI: Oh well, people say they saw Abeku leaving the castle with a girl and as you know, when such news reaches the Asafo group, we should investigate because no black woman has ever left the castle wearing a Portuguese army shirt.

ABEKU: Oh. Well, well, so what do you want to know Takyi?

TAKYI: Anything you can tell me because the

Asafo group would want to know. Do not forget we seek the welfare of this Edina town. Do not forget also that your father was an important member of the Asafo group.

ABEKU: Well my father is dead so let us leave him alone.

TAKYI: We haven't seen his body so you cannot say we should leave him in peace, for as long as we have not seen his remains and buried him, he will not have peace for himself.

ABEKU: Whatever it is, let us leave him out of this. If you want to know about the girl from the castle, you had better ask her yourself.

TAKYI: *(Turning towards Asana)* Hey girl, what's your name? *(Asana doesn't reply)* She is not answering. I'm sure you can answer for her.

ABEKU: She's called Asana. That means she's a twin.

ANIMA: Takyi, I don't think all this is necessary. Don't you see the woman is tired? She needs some rest.

TAKYI: Yes, yes, yes that's true. That is why I

wanted your brother to explain things to us.

ANIMA: What explanation do you want?

TAKYI: Well, you see, they fired the canons a while ago which meant that the slave ship was leaving. They always do that. These Portuguese are inhuman. To put your fellow human in chains and send them to a foreign land is not human. Now another ship has left with some slaves. But just before that, people saw you Abeku with this girl. So tell me simply what I want to know. Who is this girl?

ABEKU: But I told you her name. She is called Asana.

TAKYI: Was she not one of the slave girls?

ASANA: *(Angrily shouting)* I am not a slave girl. My name is Asana!

ABEREWA: Takyi don't upset the poor girl. She has had enough rough times. *(Turning to Asana)* First of all, you'll need a good bath. Then Anima will give you something decent to put on. You will also call me Mena, like my children do. From now on, you are one of us. We are going to look after you, so that you can have your baby in good health.

Anima, can you take her to go and have her bath?

ANIMA: Yes. (*To Asana*) But Asana, I see you are only wearing one earring. You lost the other one.

ASANA: I gave it to my brother.

ANIMA: You gave it to your brother? But men don't wear earrings so what did you give it to him for?

ABEKU: She is lying. On our way from the castle, she took it off and threw it into the lagoon.

ASANA: (*Vehemently*) Yes, yes, yes! I threw it into the lagoon and that was for my brother. It was to protect him. That's my sacrifice to protect my twin brother. Remember he is part of me.

ANIMA: Oh, it doesn't matter. I will get you a new pair of earrings.

ASANA: No, I don't want a new pair of earrings. I am going to wear this one.

ANIMA: Only one earring?

ASANA: Yes! Yes! Yes!

ANIMA: Alright, as you please. Now, let's go.

(Anima goes with Asana into the backyard.)

TAKYI: Now Abeku, let us go out for a drink. I am sure you have a lot to tell me about this girl because the whole Asafo group will have to know.

(As they leave, Spirit comes in and sighs regretfully.)

SPIRIT: Oh well, what is the point? I have seen Fuseini, Asana's brother and he is alright. He is immensely disturbed about his sister and has been looking for her. He has some trouble with the slave keepers, but what's the point? Nobody can hear me. Poor human beings. Poor mortals. Poor, poor mortals.

CURTAIN

ACT TWO

*(The scene is the same, the time is late afternoon. When the
curtain opens, Asana is standing in the middle of the stage
holding Aberewa's calabash and staring at the contents. She
is visibly heavy with child and obviously in some discomfort.
She is still wearing the lone copper earring. She moves to a
chair which is on the opposite side of Aberewa's room near
the cooking area. She sits down with difficulty and starts
stringing the beads. The spirit walks in, peeps at what Asana
is doing and sits down. Takyi walks in, holding a basket.)*

TAKYI: Hey Asana! How are you doing?

ASANA: *(Simply)* I don't know.

TAKYI: You are still wearing that earring.

ASANA: Yes.

TAKYI: And you are still sitting down here with
            that thing in front of you?

ASANA: What, the calabash?

TAKYI: No, your stomach. You should be having
            that baby by now. That baby is long
            overdue. You are about the same period
            as Esi and she had her baby two weeks

	ago and you are still sitting here, looking like a hen. I say, I say, when are you going to have that baby?
ASANA:	I am not going to have that baby.
TAKYI:	Are you going to keep the baby in that belly of yours forever?
ASANA:	Yes, I am not going to give birth to a white baby. That child will die in my stomach.
SPIRIT:	That means you too will die and that is suicide, stupid girl. The Portuguese will call that suicide.
TAKYI:	You are being childish. If that baby dies in your stomach, you will also die.
ASANA:	That will be good. Then all shame will come to an end.
	(After a pause) Takyi, we haven't seen you in this house for some time now.
TAKYI:	I know, I know. I have been busy with the Asafo Company preparing for the Bakatue.
ASANA:	What is Bakatue?
TAKYI:	Bakatue is an Edina festival which lifts the ban on fishing in the lagoon. Don't you know about it?

ASANA:	No, I don't know about it. What have you got in that basket?
TAKYI:	Fresh fish from the lagoon. I fetched it yesterday. I thought Anima would be at the lagoon yesterday. All fish mongers in Edina were there. Now, where is she?
ASANA:	She is in the backyard.
TAKYI:	*(Raising his voice)* Hey Anima........Anima!
ASANA:	Takyi, don't shout like that, Aberewa is asleep.
TAKYI:	*(Apologetically)* Oh sorry, sorry.....sorry.

(Anima enters from the backyard and looks angrily at Takyi.)

ANIMA:	Takyi, why do you shout like that, don't you know my mother is asleep?
TAKYI:	I said I'm sorry my dear Anima, but I brought you some fish from the lagoon. Yesterday was Bakatue, you know.
ANIMA:	Yes, I know.
TAKYI:	But you didn't come.
ANIMA:	No, I didn't come because I was busy looking after Asana. She could have her baby at any time. Anyway, let me look at the fish you brought me.

26

(She takes the basket from Takyi and inspects the fish in it.)

Very nice fish.

TAKYI: *(Pleased with himself)* Oh yes, yes. Only the best is good enough for you.

ANIMA: How much?

TAKYI: This is a gift from me.

ANIMA: Takyi, you haven't given up.

TAKYI: No, I will not give up. I want you to marry me.

ANIMA: And you want to buy me off with fish from the lagoon.

TAKYI: *(Angrily)* No Anima, now you are being difficult and you make me feel like a beggar. I don't like it. I tell you, I don't like it.

(Aberewa enters the stage from her room.)

TAKYI: Oh Aberewa, you are awake.

SPIRIT: Of course she's awake. You were shouting!

ABEREWA: *(Sleepily)* Yes. Takyi is that you? I heard your voice.

ANIMA: You see, I told you, you would wake her up. You and your loud voice.

27

ABEREWA:	*(Sitting down in front of her room)* We haven't seen you for some time.
TAKYI:	That's true Aberewa. But the Asafo Company was busy at the shrine preparing for Bakatue. We prayed and poured libation to the gods of the sea and lagoon for them to grant all our wishes.
ABEREWA:	Oh yes, that was yesterday. I heard the singing and drumming all night.
TAKYI:	Oh yes, we were singing......... *(Starts singing)*
	Obrumankoma *Obrumankoma* *Obrumankoma ee....!*
ABEREWA:	Enough! Enough, Takyi. I had enough of that noise last night.
TAKYI:	*(Crestfallen)* Oh Aberewa, I was going to sing you that song..... especially for you.
ABEREWA:	Thank you very much. But was it a good festival?
TAKYI:	*(Proudly)* Oh, yes......yes. There were many people. There were chiefs and visitors from the other towns and the place was very lively. When finally the ban was lifted from the Benya lagoon, there was a very big catch, a bumper

harvest. I brought some fish to Anima. She couldn't come to the festival and she tells me she was busy looking after this pregnant woman.

ABEREWA: Yes, the baby was due some days ago and I don't know why that baby has delayed for so long.

TAKYI: But do you know Aberewa, the woman tells me she is not going to have her baby, and that she will die with the baby in her stomach rather than give birth to it.

ABEREWA: Is that what you said?

ASANA: *(Softly)* Yes Aberewa.

ABEREWA: That's very naughty. A pregnant woman shouldn't talk like that. You have been bathed with water from the lagoon and that should make you strong to have your baby and keep your life and your sanity. So stop talking like that.

SPIRIT: This girl is stubborn, but she will get over it.

ANIMA: You know Mena, that Asana has not been taking her medicine and she quarrels with me and tells me that I shouldn't treat her like a slave.

ABEREWA: Oh Asana! Is that what you said?

29

ASANA:	Yes I said that.
SPIRIT:	You see, I said this girl is stubborn.
ABEREWA:	You should not. Asana, you should not speak like that. Nobody in this house treats you like a slave. And that is not the way to speak.
ASANA:	I am sorry, Aberewa.
ABEREWA:	You should learn to call me Mena. Now, you should take you medicine seriously. All pregnant women take medicines and if they don't they have difficulty in childbirth. It is not a good thing to wish your baby to die in your stomach. That is a taboo in Edina and now that you are my daughter, you shouldn't talk like that.
ASANA:	*(Suddenly gnashes her teeth and groans with pain)* Oh my stomach! Oh my stomach!
SPIRIT:	Aha!!
TAKYI:	Aha! Time is getting closer. She is going to have a baby!
ANIMA:	Now you shut up.
	(Spirit laughs).
	This is not for men to interfere. I think you should go and leave the women to sort it out.

ABEREWA: Anima, why don't you take her inside to rest?

ANIMA: *(Turning to Asana)* Give me the calabash. *(She takes it and gives it to Takyi)* You hold this! Asana, let's go, you need to rest.

(Anima takes Asana into her room to rest and closes the door. Takyi examines the beads in the calabash with his fingers as Abeku walks onto the stage.)

SPIRIT: My son, you have to be careful with your movements. If these white bastards get to find out what you are up to they will string you like meat and roast you like kyikyinga.

ABEREWA: Oh Abeku, you have closed early today.

ABEKU: Yes Mena, a new ship sailed in and the governor let us all go home early.

ABEREWA: Oh! Have they come to take new prisoners?

ABEKU: There are no prisoners at the castle.

ABEREWA: So what is the ship for then?

ABEKU: This ship doesn't look like a slave ship and the captain doesn't look like a slave trader.

SPIRIT: He is not. He is just another European adventurer floating on the sea looking for

31

a place to land. Christopher Columbus, the Spanish explorer, was doing similar things; stopping over at the Elmina Castle many many years ago, and landed at the West Indies.

ABEKU: Mena, the governor has been talking to me about Asana. You know, that governor seems to like Asana.

SPIRIT: Of course he does, the bastard! He slept with her.

ABEKU: Now he wants to know when she is going to have the baby.

ABEREWA: And what did you tell him?

ABEKU: Well, Mena........Mena...How would I know? You would know. You are the.........eh, you know......you know.

SPIRIT: Say midwife!!

ABEKU: By the way, how is she?

ABEREWA: Well, it looks like her time is getting closer. That girl is stubborn. She doesn't want to have the baby.

ABEKU: So what does she want to do with the pregnancy?

ABEREWA: She wants to kill the baby.

TAKYI: No! She must not do that. But Aberewa,

I want to say something.

ABEREWA: Yes Takyi, let me hear you.

TAKYI: Aberewa, I don't like the way Anima treats me.

ABEREWA: Oh?

TAKYI: She doesn't treat me good. She doesn't treat me like a man.

ABEREWA: Oh, don't mind Anima. She is just teasing you. That girl is always like that. You should know it by now.

TAKYI: I don't want to be teased. I am a man. I think somebody should tell Anima that.

ABEKU: *(With a laugh)* I will tell her myself.

(Anima emerges from the room and goes to Aberewa.)

ANIMA: Mena I do not hear any sound, the baby is silent.

ABEREWA: Oh Anima, you worry too much. Maybe the baby is asleep. The womb can be very comfortable and babies like their comfort.

ANIMA: I don't think so, and I think you should come and look at it yourself.

(Aberewa gets up and makes her way gingerly into the room, followed by Anima. Takyi shakes the calabash with the beads and tries to make a rhythm with it.)

33

TAKYI: Abeku, your mother is a wonderful woman.

SPIRIT: Of course she is wonderful, that is why I married her.

ABEKU: Why do you say that?

TAKYI: Well, your mother cannot see because she is blind but she is able to work and string these beads as if she can see.

SPIRIT: Of course, of course. *(He walks off the stage)*

ABEKU: Yes, she has been working with the beads for a long time, long before she became blind.

TAKYI: And I also know that she is a good mid-wife and pregnant women come to seek her advice.

ABEKU: Yes, yes, she was delivering pregnant women in their homes. She has been going out to deliver pregnant women in their homes, even when she became blind. Yes, she was doing all that, but stopped when my father died but now that Asana is here; it is only natural that she would take care of her.

TAKYI: But I hear the baby is not moving.

ABEKU: Yes, yes that was what Anima said. *(Raising his voice)* Yes, yes Takyi, but what is all this?

TAKYI: Oh, I am worried. Does it mean the baby is dead in the belly?

ABEKU: I don't know.

TAKYI: That means Asana will also die.

ABEKU: I don't know.

TAKYI: Maybe the baby is not dead.

ABEKU: Maybe.

TAKYI: Maybe Asana will not also die.

ABEKU: Maybe.

TAKYI: Maybe the baby will be born alive.

ABEKU: Maybe.

TAKYI: Will the governor marry her?

ABEKU: No.

TAKYI: Will you marry her?

ABEKU: *(Raising his voice)* No no no!

TAKYI: But she is a nice girl?

ABEKU: Yes, she is a nice girl but I am not going to marry her. Could you imagine me, a black man like me, married to a black woman like Asana, and she carrying a white baby on her back? People will laugh at me, carrying a white baby, a Portuguese baby, people will laugh at me. I am the son of my father, you know Takyi, and I am a proud African.

TAKYI: Do they know that they killed your father?

ABEKU: No.

TAKYI: Do they know that they once fired their big guns and some fishermen died?

ABEKU: No, they don't care. The lives of black people don't matter to them.

TAKYI: But you work for them.

ABEKU: I have my reasons. These Portuguese think they can come to Edina, build their castle and use it for slaves and for keeping big guns. They will see.

TAKYI: What will they see? You have not got big guns. You Africans don't have guns.

ABEKU: Africans do not have big guns but some other white people have guns. You wait and see.

TAKYI: *(Giving him the calabash with beads)* You Abeku, I think you are crazy, crazy, crazy... *(He walks off the stage)*

36

(Left alone, Abeku walks aimlessly and stops in the middle of the stage.)

ABEKU: Crazy? *(Cynical laughter)* I'm not crazy…I. Am. Not. Crazy. I am angry. I am very angry! If these white people at the castle, these Portuguese explode their big guns and kill my father, smashing him to pieces so that we can't even find his body to bury; with his ghost probably roaming about haunting people like a restless spirit without a resting place; then I have to be angry.

I am a Wednesday born and I'm going to wear the cloak of the devil and the devil never forgives. That is why I, Kweku Bonsam, am not going to forgive the Portuguese in the castle. I am going to avenge my father's death. And that is why I cannot forgive our elders who gave them permission to come and build a castle here in Edina. They must have told them they wanted to come and settle here for business but they have turned the place into a slave market and that makes me angry. So if other white men who also have big guns, plan to fight the Portuguese, then I will help them.

I am angry because they capture and drive these slaves from afar, far beyond the borders of this country like a herd of cattle and come and dump them in the castle and put them in chains like animals, and sleep with them at will and make them pregnant then throw them away.

Look at Asana, she is expecting that baby but she doesn't want to release the baby. The baby is probably dead in her stomach. Who knows, probably she will also die. That is why I am angry. That is why the people of Edina should be angry like me.

(He puts the calabash down near Aberewa's chair and sits on the chair. Anima comes out of the room, Abeku gets up in anticipation.)

ANIMA: Where is Takyi?

ABEKU: He is gone. How is Asana?

ANIMA: Fetch us some water.

(As he goes to fetch the water, a baby starts crying.
Aberewa calls "Anima, where is the water"
Anima says "Hurry up",
Spirit rushes unto the stage. He hops about the stage shouting "It's a boy! It's a boy! It's a boy!")

CURTAIN

ACT THREE

(The scene is the same. Aberewa is sitting on her favourite chair stringing beads. After a while she calls Asana but Asana doesn't reply.)

ABEREWA: *(Raising her voice)* Asana! *(Still no reply).*

ABEREWA: *(Shouts)* Asana!!

ASANA: *(Offstage.........Sleepily)* Aberewa *(She comes out of the room rubbing her eyes sleepily.)*

ABEREWA: Were you asleep?

ASANA: Yes Aberewa.

ABEREWA: You still call me Aberewa. You are a stubborn girl.

ASANA: I'm sorry Aberewa.....Oh! I'm sorry Mena.

ABEREWA: You should be celebrating the outdooring of your child and not sleeping like that. Come here, these new beads are for you. I want to put them around you.

ASANA: But you put one round my waist already.

ABEREWA: That one is different. In our culture, women who come of age ought to put

39

these beads around their waists. The men also like to play with it. But the one I gave you was to strengthen you to have the baby. Now, just keep quiet and come here. *(Aberewa puts the big white beads round her neck)* There! Now, you should be ashamed of yourself.

ASANA: I'm sorry Aberewa, but I am not.

ABEREWA: You will be one day. That baby is your child and he lived in your womb for nine whole months and your blood is flowing in his veins.

ASANA: *(Shrugging her shoulders)* That makes me laugh... ha ha ha!! Some blood......some veins.

ABEREWA: You ought to be ashamed of yourself. Asana, you ought to be ashamed of yourself. You don't even know where your baby is.

ASANA: I don't care. You all care but I don't. As far as I am concerned, that child can die and I will not shed a tear.

ABEREWA: You are so bitter that the tears in your eyes are dried up, so that even when I die, there will be none to shed for me.

ASANA: Oh Aberewa, don't say that. You will never die.

40

ABEREWA: Now you make me laugh. I should be laughing at your naivety. God created all of us to live on this earth and to die on this earth. I am still mourning my husband because I know he is dead. But pity is that, since we have not seen his body to give him a burial, his spirit is still roaming around.

SPIRIT: I am not roaming around; I am standing right here by you.

ASANA: Do all ghosts roam around?

ABEREWA: No, only those who have no burial roam about reckless and disturbed and cause a lot of havoc.

SPIRIT: Oh! I don't cause any harm. I am a happy spirit. I am happy because I can go where I want to go, see what I want to see and learn what I want to learn.

ABEREWA: You are still young. You will grow up and learn the full value of life. That is why when you have a baby you should love it and care for it. You do not even know where your child is.

ASANA: *(Shouting)* No! No! No! Aberewa no!

ABEREWA: Asana you are shouting.

ASANA: *(Shouting)* Yes, yes, I am shouting.

41

Aberewa, I want to shout. I want to scream at all of you because you make me want to shout. *(Now sobering down)* Oh Aberewa, I am sorry, I am sorry but it hurts so much here *(points to her chest)* my heart.

ABEREWA: I will not blame you for wanting to shout. I know that you are passing through difficult times, but that is life. We all pass through difficult times but you should not let them crack you like a calabash.

ASANA: Calabash is useful.

ABEREWA: *(With a laugh)* I know, Asana, I know. Calabash is used for fetching water; the men use it for drinking palm wine and for pouring libation. You put food into a calabash and you eat from it. Beggars use it for begging. You put cowries and other valuables into it for safe keeping. They also use it for making music. I put my beads into it before I string them. It is a delicate thing, but you are a woman and a woman is not a calabash so you must be strong and must not allow yourself to crack like a calabash. Do you understand what I am saying Asana?

ASANA: Yes, I do.

ABEREWA: Good. Now, every woman should be like
            the ant hill.

ASANA: Ant hill?

ABEREWA: Yes, the ant hill is firm and strong. It
            stands alone in the field. It has no roof,
            it has no clothing, It stands naked. The
            rain falls on it all the time and yet it never
            dissolves or melts. The sun shines on it
            every day but it doesn't crack. The storm
            invades it and the wind blows at it all
            the time, but it never falls. And inside it
            are ants. Many, many ants of all colours
            roam about, it is their home. Now Asana,
            do you understand that too?

ASANA: *(Shaking her head)* No.

ABEREWA: Oh well, never mind. You are young
            and you are still growing up. Maybe
            someday...someday...

            Now I will tell you where your child is.
            That baby is with Esi, Anima's friend.
            She also delivered a baby boy two weeks
            before you and she has big breasts and
            therefore plenty of milk for two.

ASANA: *(Cynically)* Hmmm......Good for her.

ABEREWA: What about your breasts? They should
            be getting full by now and you must not
            be spilling it out. That's a stupid thing

43

to do especially when that is meant for your child.

They are having the outdooring ceremony today. Outdooring in our tradition is very important for mother and child. And every child, no matter the parents, is a gift from God. Listen Asana, when nature prepares a future for you and God blesses it, then you need to be thankful to everybody. The God on high, the gods of our ancestors, the sea, the lagoon and the earth. That is why you should be at your own outdooring. Anyway, Anima has been at the ceremony since morning and I reckon by this time they must have finished.

SPIRIT: Yes, I was there. I saw them, they've finished.

(Anima enters. She is dressed in white.)

ANIMA: Hey Asana, you should have been at the outdooring of your own child, not me. Look at you, just look at you. You look pretty even though you are still wearing one earring.

SPIRIT: This woman is stubborn.

ABEREWA: Anima, what happened? How did the ceremony go?

ANIMA: *(With excitement)* It was exciting! It was wonderful! Oh Mena, it was beautiful! Nothing you can think of. Everybody was asking about the mother and here you are sitting down grumbling and grumbling. You should have been there. There was Esi holding two babies in her arms: one black, one white and both of them were feeding from her breasts. I do not know what you are doing with your breast milk but very soon you will be wetting yourself with it.

ABEREWA: So what did they call him?

ANIMA: They wanted to call him by the governor's name but they didn't know his name so they called him Kweku Broni.

SPIRIT: I can get the name for you. But what's the point? You can't see me, you can't hear me.

ABEREWA Well, we can get the white man's name. We can ask Abeku to find out because the child must bear the name of the father. What about Esi's husband?

ANIMA: Oh that man was as happy as a goat. He was proud that his wife was giving breast milk to two babies - one black, one white. And the man got himself drunk

45

as if he was responsible for both babies. You should be ashamed of yourself. You should have been feeding that baby yourself.

ASANA: But I warned you when you tried to force me to breastfeed him that I would cut off my breasts. And I meant it. I was not going to give any part of my body to any bastard. You people don't understand me. That man forced me and slept with me. He did not only do that, he humiliated me. He would first strip me naked and sketch me.

SPIRIT: Oh yes, that governor is a crazy artist. He paints. I think he was fond of Asana. You would even say that he was in love with Asana.

ASANA: When he got to know that I was pregnant, he stopped sleeping with me but he would first call me, strip me naked and ask me to do all sorts of things so that he could sketch.

SPIRIT: That governor is still painting from the sketches of Asana. That man is crazy.

ANIMA: Oh, you should have seen the gifts people brought: yam, fish, palm oil, plantain,

46

and cocoyam. They had wanted to give them to me for Asana but I refused.

ASANA: That's your choice.

ANIMA: Hey Asana, do you know something?

ASANA: (*She says angrily*) I don't know anything.

ANIMA: You are always angry.

ASANA: Yes, I am angry, always angry.

ANIMA: Asana, do you remember the queen-mother who visited you when you were pregnant? Are you angry with her too?

ASANA: (*Suddenly brightening up*) Oh no, she was a kindly woman, I remember her, and now that I am fine, I think I should go and visit her.

ANIMA: Well, she heard about your outdooring, and she sent a present to you.

ASANA: She sent me a present, the queenmother?

ANIMA: She sent you a pair of earrings.

ASANA: (*Confused*) But…..but...

ANIMA: There should be no buts with the queenmother. She orders that you should give her your earring; she will put it on her shrine and pray for the safety of your entire family. Now you

47

will wear a pair of earrings like every
woman in this town.

ASANA: (*Ponders and sighs*) Oh that sounds good.
That queenmother is a good woman.

ANIMA: That settles it.

ABEREWA: Asana, you are a lucky woman. The
queenmother is fond of you. From now
on you should behave like every other
woman in Edina.

*(They exchange earrings; Abeku rushes onto the stage and
without greeting anyone, rushes into Aberewa's room and
immediately comes out panting.)*

ABEKU: They've found him! They've found him!

ANIMA: They've found who?

ABEKU: Mena, where is my father's Asafo dress?

ANIMA: But you are not a member of the Asafo
group. What do you want the Asafo
dress for?

ABEKU: (*Ignoring her*) Mena, where is my father's
Asafo dress?

ABEREWA: It is in my room. What do you want it
for?

(Abeku does not answer but goes into the room.)

SPIRIT: Oh dear, at long last.

(Abeku presently comes back with a red dress.)

ABEKU: Now they've found my father, I can take
            his place in the Asafo group.

(He enters his room.)

ANIMA: Where did they find him?

*(Takyi rushes onto the stage excited and panting heavily. He
is wearing a red Asafo dress and holding a bracelet).*

TAKYI: Anima, Anima look at this. Do you rec-
            ognise this bracelet?

(Anima is shocked and covers her eyes with her hands.)

ANIMA: Show it to Mena.

TAKYI: But Aberewa cannot see.

ANIMA: *(Angrily)* I know that! But give it to her!

ABEREWA: Takyi, give me that thing!

*(Takyi gives the bracelet to Aberewa. She takes the bracelet
and presses it to her bosom.)*

ABEREWA: *(Sighs)* At last.

TAKYI: You do recognise it don't you?

ABEREWA: Yes I do Takyi, I bought it myself. I gave
            it to him when we just got married.

(Spirit slumps onto the floor and sits down in Buddhist fashion.)

TAKYI: That settles it. Now we know that we've found the remains of your husband and they are taking him to the cemetery for burial so you keep this.

ABEREWA: No, take it along and bury him with it.

TAKYI: But this is gold. Pure gold.

ABEREWA: Yes I know, I know. I bought it myself and I gave it to him because he was my husband. And even though he's dead and you've found his bones, he is still my husband and this gold bracelet belongs to him because he still is my husband and he must carry this bracelet even into his grave.

SPIRIT: I should be crying, but nobody will see me. This woman was very fond of me. I did not realise this when I was alive.

(He buries his head in his hands.)

TAKYI: Alright then, we should bury him with his gold bracelet.

(Abeku comes out wearing a red dress.)

TAKYI: Hey Abeku, this is your father's Asafo dress.

ABEKU:	Yes Takyi. From today on I should be a member of the Asafo group. I'm taking the place of my father.
TAKYI:	Well, we asked you to join and you wouldn't.
ABEKU:	I know, but now I will.
TAKYI:	Abeku, let's go to the cemetery because they should be digging the grave by now.
ANIMA:	But where did you find him?
TAKYI:	They found him somewhere in the rocks, the sea must have washed his remains there. Aberewa, I'm going to sing you that Asafo song.
ABEREWA:	Alright, Takyi.

(Takyi starts singing the song and Abeku joins him.)

Call:	*Obrumankoma*
	Obrumankoma
	Obrumankoma ee!
Response:	*Obrumankoma ee!*
Call:	*Obrumankoma,*
	Odapangyan ee!
Response:	*Obrumankoma,*

Odapagyan ee!
Oson ei!
Oson akyir nnyi aboa!

(When they finish, Takyi says to Abeku)

TAKYI: Abeku shall we go?

ABEKU: Yes, let's go.

(As they leave, Anima calls Takyi.)

ANIMA: Takyi.

TAKYI: Yes Anima.

ANIMA: Shall I come to the cemetery too?

TAKYI: This business is for men so you better stay home for the time being.

ANIMA: Takyi, the man you are going to bury is my father.........Now, please Takyi.

(Takyi hesitates, sighs heavily and stretches his hand towards Anima. Anima takes his hand and they both leave.)

ABEREWA: *(Sighs thoughtfully)* This old man God up there has his way of doing things.

ASANA: I am sorry Aberewa, and I sympathise with you.

ABEREWA: Don't feel sorry for me Asana. You see I'm not crying......I'm not shedding tears. In fact, I'm happy today because they found the remains of my husband. I am happy because he will find a place to rest forever. I am happy because his spirit will not roam restlessly.

SPIRIT: Oh my God, I was enjoying my situation as a roaming spirit who could go anywhere I liked. Now I can't do that anymore. *(Shivering)* Oh my God, I am feeling cold *(An eerie wind blows onto the stage. He gets up and stalks around like someone dazed and finally stumbles off stage.)*

ABEREWA: .... I must celebrate today. Asana, I want you to be happy because I am happy.

ASANA: Yes Aberewa.

ABEREWA: Now that my husband has been found, I should start wearing something white.

ASANA: In that case, you can have my cover cloth. I don't need to wear white *(She puts her cover cloth around Aberewa's shoulders.)*

ABEREWA: Asana, today I want to look pretty.

ASANA: Yes Aberewa. You already look pretty.

ABEREWA: *(Laughing)* You are kind Asana, but I must look more pretty. I want you to make my hair............now.

ASANA: Yes Aberewa.

ABEREWA: You are really stubborn. You still call me
            Aberewa. I know it is difficult, but I want
            you to regard me as your mother. I want
            to sit on the floor and you to sit on the
            chair behind me like I used to do when
            I was a child.

ASANA: Yes Mena, but let me get a comb from
            our room.

*(She goes into her room. Aberewa gets up and sits on the
ground. She spreads both hands on the floor and chants in
mirth.)*

> I like to touch the ground
> I like to feel the earth
> The earth likes all of me
> The earth will make me happy again
> Happy, Happy again *(She laughs).*

(Asana emerges from the room with a comb in her hand.)

ASANA: You sound very happy.

ABEREWA: I told you today is a happy day for me.

ASANA: How do you want your hair done?

ABEREWA: Anything you think will make me pretty.

*(Asana sits on the chair behind her, parts her hair with her
fingers and begins to weave it.)*

ABEREWA: Asana, I'm going to tell you something.

ASANA: Yes Mena. And I am going to listen to you.

ABEREWA: *(Laughs)* I'm glad you are now calling me Mena.

ASANA: Yes, yes Mena *(They both laugh)*.

ABEREWA: Good. We are all children of God. Both white and black but we live on different lands. Very soon we shall live on the same land. The white man is now living on our land and producing their children, like yours. I believe that one day our people who have been captured as slaves and taken away will produce their children in the white man's land and their children will be strong and powerful like the white man. I believe that this slave trade will one day come to an end and the black man in the white man's land shall rise and rise and rise. I also believe that the white man's child here in Edina will rise and rise and rise. That is why we should accept everything that happens to us as our destiny. Asana, do you believe in destiny?

ASANA: Mena, I do not know anything about that

but my mother used to tell me that there is a future for everybody. Is that what they call destiny?

ABEREWA: Yes. When nature prepares your future and the Almighty approves, it becomes your destiny. So....so....so....

ASANA: So Mena you are telling me that I should accept that this is my destiny? For your sake I will *(She giggles)*. Mena, sometimes you talk like my mother. When I was small, my mother used to tell me 'Asana, one day you will grow up into a nice woman and many men will want to marry you and the man who will marry you will have many cattle and he will be nice to you. You will give him many children including twins like you and your twin brother Fuseini' *(She giggles)*. But that was just a dream. Now my situation is not a dream, it is reality and the reality is that my womanhood has been abused and that reality makes me angry and I hate the white man for it, and I cannot forgive him. But I will not crack like a calabash. Suddenly I have grown up and I am going to be strong like your anthill. *(She giggles)*

And for your sake I will take my child

back and let him feed at my breasts. I will
look after him, knowing that one day he
will also be strong and rise and rise and
rise. And will be a good citizen of Edina.
Isn't that what you want, Mena?

(Aberewa does not reply)
Mena, isn't that what you want?

(Aberewa still does not reply)

Mena!....Mena!...Mena!

*(When Aberewa does not reply, Asana shakes her and finds
that she is limp. She looks at her and closes her eyelids.
We hear the horn of a ship blowing in the distance. Asana
listens.)*

ASANA: Now, that is the horn of the ship. That
              ship is sailing away to sea. There are no
              slaves on that ship so that ship will fire
              no guns but it will only blow its horn.
              But Mena will not hear that sound.

*(Asana strokes Aberewa's head tenderly and suddenly
screams.)*
Menaaa!!

CURTAIN